Mary Peake and the Mighty Acorn

By DAVID MESSICK

Illustrated by Liu Light

Mary Peake and the Mighty Acorn

© 2019 / All Rights Reserved
Text David Messick
Original Art Lui Light
Puppet Images Rainbow Productions, Inc.

ISBN: 978-1-733-24841-9

Printed in the USA

Third Printing
Rainbow Puppet Publications
18 Easthill Court
Hampton, Virginia 23664

www.rainbowpuppets.com   info@rainbowpuppets.com
Rainbow Puppet Productions, Inc. is a non-profit,
educational, entertainment company

Designed by Lynn Mangosing

Special thanks to Curtis Johnson, Ruth Manlove, Traci Massie,
Courtney Seaborne, and Rose West at Optima Health.

To my Dad…

…who shared his love of history with me and who introduced me to the story of the Emancipation Oak and a teacher from Hampton.

Contents

"Mighty Trees from Little Acorns Grow"

Adapted from Chaucer

In 1831, a law was passed in Virginia that made the instruction of reading to any black person in the state, whether free or enslaved, against the law. There were severe fines and punishments for anyone who failed to follow that law.

Fortunately, two things happened that same year. A little girl was learning how to read in the District of Columbia and a little acorn had just taken root in a place we now call **Hampton, Virginia.**

This is the story of that little girl and that tiny acorn...

For the Love of Education

Mary Kelsey loves Sunday more than any other day of the week. As always, she's up extra early and has already put on the blue dress, with flowers on the front. It's one of her favorites.

But it's not the pretty dresses that Mary is most excited about. She loves school and at five years old, she only gets to go to school on Sundays. Every week, before the church service, there is Sunday School for Mary and her friends.

"I wonder what stories we'll hear today? Maybe Jonah and the big fish. Or maybe it will be David and the giant **Goliath**," she said to her mother. "Hurry up, we'll be late."

"Mary, we don't have to be there for another hour and a half. Now come down here. It's time for breakfast," said her mother from the kitchen.

"I can't wait to learn how to read. Then I can pick the stories just like Mrs. Wilson does."

"So, you're going to be a teacher?" asked Mary's mother.

"Maybe, but first I'll have to go school every day. I'll dress up, and get to walk down the street to the school, and meet with all my friends."

Mary's mother sighed. She'd been avoiding telling Mary about her decision, but Mary was almost six years old and it seemed today would be the day.

"Well Mary, I've got great news for you. We've found a wonderful school for you, in **Alexandria**."

"Alexandria? That's where Aunt Mary lives. Why would I go to school there?"

"Because there are no schools here in **Norfolk**."

"Of course, there are, we walk past one every time we go to the market," said Mary.

"Mary, we have discussed this before. You know *that*

school is only for white children. You can't go there."

"But my father's white. Doesn't that count for something?" said Mary.

"Not in the eyes of the law."

Mary Smith Kelsey was born in Norfolk, Virginia in 1823, and Virginia was very different then. The United States of America was very different as well. While the nation had been founded under the idea that all were free, that was hardly true.

Most black Americans were enslaved, forced to work for others with no say of their own. They were concentrated in southern states like Virginia. Most slave holders in America believed that reading, writing, and any other education for their slaves was a dangerous thing that could lead to reading maps, learning ways to escape, or perhaps rising up against their captors.

Mary's mother was not enslaved, she was a "free person of color." Her father was a well-to-do white man from Europe. In the eyes of the laws at that time, even a mixed-race child like Mary was considered black. That meant very limited educational opportunities existed for her in Norfolk.

In 1829, Alexandria was part of the District of Columbia, and not subject to the harsh education laws of Virginia. Girls like Mary could go to school there.

"What if I tried really hard? I could be as smart as those children."

Her mother sighed, "Mary, this has nothing to do with how smart you are. If that were it, you'd be at the top of any class in Norfolk or anywhere else."

"But why do you want me to go away? Don't you love me?"

Mary's mom grabbed her and hugged her as hard as she could. "I love you more than anything. I only want the best for you. And you can't have that here. That's why you're going to Alexandria. But you know, not a day will go by that I won't be thinking of you and praying for you. And I expect to get lots of letters from you so I know that you are working hard. Will you do that?

"I will Mama. I will," said Mary.

Life in Alexandria

Mary did work hard. She arrived at school already knowing her A, B, C's better than anyone else in the class. When she would go out to play with her friends, she would lead them in singing those A, B, C's with her beautiful voice.

Mary also had the ability to explain things to others in a way that could be easily understood. So, when any of her friends struggled in class, Mary could help them by explaining in a simple and clear way.

Soon, Mary was reading. And she couldn't get enough to read. She would read her school book, or **primer** as it was called, cover to cover. And no sooner did she finish reading than she would go back to the beginning and start all over again.

With her new-found skills, she was writing in no time. She was also learning troubling news about her home state and the country.

In Southampton County, Virginia, Nat Turner and other enslaved people rebelled against their treatment and revolted. Newspapers reported that over 50 people were dead.

That rebellion terrified slave holders who felt that slaves who could read and write would be a danger to the community. They would be able to read escape maps and they would be able to forge papers that would allow them to travel to freedom.

Virginia passed a law making it illegal for any black person, whether enslaved or free, to learn how to read or write.

Mary thought of her friends in Norfolk. She thought of her church school where her friends had been learning to read from the Bible. All that had to end because there were **vigilantes** who would spy and report any black people who were learning to read or write.

Mary then thought of how smart her mother had been in sending her to Alexandria. She was now learning, not only for herself but for her friends who were denied that right. This made her study and work all the harder.

But it wasn't just reading that she learned. Remember those beautiful dresses that Mary loved to look at and wear? She was learning to make those dresses in sewing classes. She was also learning fine needlework skills. She was most happy that she could combine her love of reading and sewing in the same class.

"Mary, that is the most beautiful sampler I've ever seen a young lady make. Come class, take a look. This is how you are to do your needlework." And at that, Mary's teacher picked up the cloth on which Mary was hand sewing the letter 'D.'"

In Mary's school, every young lady was expected to learn embroidered needlework, showing off their skill with a 'sampler' of their work. Mary has stitched the A, B, C's on her sampler and had then gone a step further. Below each letter she sewed a picture. Under the 'A' is an apple, under the 'B' is a bird, under the 'C' is a cat.

Her teacher then exclaimed, "Why, even when my eyesight was perfect, I couldn't have made such even stitches."

A young girl beside Mary sighed, "I wish I could sew as good as you do, Mary."

"Here Amelia, let me show you," said Mary. And at that, Mary helped Amelia make perfect stitches.

As much as Mary loved sewing, reading remained her great joy. A good book could take her away to faraway places she had never heard of before. Or, it could tell about the lives of famous people who lived long ago. But there was one book she cherished more than any other, and that was her Bible.

She had been introduced to Bible stories back when she lived with her mother in Norfolk. Now, with her aunt, church became the place she'd meet new friends and hear about her community. As an excellent reader, Mary would often be called to read aloud to others. But she didn't just read; as she grew older, she had memorized many stories and many verses that she shared…

"Do to others as you would have them do to you."

"Love one another."

"For I was hungry and you gave me something to eat,
I was thirsty and you gave me something to drink,
I was a stranger and you invited me in…
I needed clothes and you clothed me."

All of these sayings helped shape the person Mary was becoming.

Mary felt safe at school. But she knew that the world was very different beyond the walls of her school.

Mary's aunt rented her home from Rollins Fowle, a **merchant** who hated slavery and did as much as he could to help others. When families were at risk of **separation**, he would try to free them and help them to start a new life. He had done that for Mary's uncle, John Paine.

Again and again, Mr. Fowle would say, "This cannot continue. Half of the states in America think slavery is wrong and want it to stop. The other half says that they have a right as **independent** states to do as they choose. Slavery is tearing this country apart!"

In 1839, it looked like the slave owning states were going to win out. Voters in the U.S. Congress passed a law that made Virginia's reading laws apply in the District of Columbia, including Alexandria.

Suddenly it was against the law for Mary, or any black American, to go to school in the nation's capital. She was devastated.

Helping Others

Mary was sad that school had ended but she was glad to be back home with her mother in Norfolk. While she had been away learning to read and write, her neighbors had a far different life with far fewer advantages.

She joined the First Baptist Church on Bute Street. Her skills were noticed by the members immediately. If there was a need for a beautiful voice in the choir, she was there. If there was a need for choir robes, she had the skills to make them.

Word soon spread of Mary's skills and she became a much-sought-after maker of all kinds of clothing. She soon had quite a business operating from her mother's home. People would come by needing a new dress for church, or pants for work, or a new shirt. Mary could handle it all.

One day, there was a knock on the door and Mary set down her sewing to answer. She was certainly startled by the sight on her mother's front porch.

"Are you Miss Mary?" said the old man at the door. He was white haired, had rough beard stubble on his face, and the rags he was wearing indicated that he was certainly someone in need.

After a moment Mary responded, "I'm Mary Kelsey. May I help you?"

"You don't know me, Miss Mary. But I sure hear a lot about you. They say you can sew most anything."

"I can sew a bit," she responded.

"I used to sew a bit," he said has he held up his wrinkled and weathered hands. "Used to mend ship sails when I could get the work. Now, these old eyes don't do me a bit of good. That's why I came by. See, this button ripped off my jacket and…"

"Oh, I can help you with that," said Mary.

"I just need the needle threaded. If there is hole in that thing, I sure can't see it."

"I'll fix it. I insist," said Mary as she ran inside for a needle and thread.

She immediately began to work on replacing the button. There was something about the old man that drew Mary to him. He was a kind spirit.

"You sure do know how to handle a needle and thread," he said as she worked away... first replacing the button and then sewing patches on the elbows which had worn through long ago.

The whole time, the old man shared stories of old Norfolk, of life on the water, and of his many adventures.

"You should write a book," said Mary.

"Wouldn't do me much good. Even if I knew how to write I couldn't read with these eyes," he said.

"But I'd read it. I could read it to you," she said.

He smiled, "I'll bet you could."

Mary took the man to her heart. She learned that he lived in a small one-room home down by the waterfront. It had a beat-up stove that could heat the room and cook a little food, whenever he had any food to cook or any wood for fuel.

Mary would show up regularly, always bringing a little food and, on cold days, some wood for the stove. She also would bring a book, usually her Bible and she'd share a story or two.

"We must be the two luckiest people alive," he'd say to Mary in the tiny little room. "You got the gift of reading, and I got the gift of hearing! Your mother sure was smart to send you off to school. That's a gift most children will never get."

"Let's pray that's not true," said Mary.

And Mary's visits continued until the day the old man died. Imagine her surprise when she learned he had left all of his possessions to her.

There, in a small box, was everything the old man owned... a few fish hooks, seven coins, a handkerchief, and button.

It may not have looked like much to anyone else, but to Mary, the lesson was great. She had shared a little time and a few stories. He was grateful for her visits and yet, she was just as grateful for the time they had shared. Helping others made her feel good.

And her sharing a little time had meant everything to the old man. He had taught Mary a lasting lesson. One that followed her when she moved from Norfolk.

Mary's mother met and married Thomas Walker and in 1851, and they moved across the Chesapeake Bay from Norfolk to what is now called Hampton, Virginia. Mary quickly found a new church home and quickly saw that there was great need in that community as well.

Mary took charge. When she was with other young women her age she said, "We need to be doing more for the people in our town. You heard the pastor this morning, he read, 'From everyone who has been given much, much will be demanded,'" she recited.

"Given much?" questioned one girl. "We aren't living like kings and queens here!"

"And I sure don't have more than three pennies in my purse," laughed another.

"That's three pennies more than I have!" said another.

"*For I was hungry and you gave me something to eat… I needed clothes and you clothed me,*" Mary recited. "We've heard that one too. Now I don't have much but I sure know how to sew. Give me any old piece of thrown-away fabric and I'll turn it into shirts in an instant. And your family has had a good crop this year. I heard your father talking about it. We might not be able to offer a lot, but we can offer a little," and Mary told of her old friend in Norfolk. "We might not be able to offer fancy food but we can offer soup."

"I can't sew, but I sure can cook!" said one of the girls. "My grandmother taught me how to throw anything we had in a pot and turn it into the best stew in town."

And so, the Daughters of Zion was founded. Under Mary's leadership, the girls were able to provide many gifts to their community including food and clothing. They were making quite a difference for the community. But there was another gift that would make an even greater difference.

Teaching in Secret

Thomas Walker, Mary's stepfather, was a leader in the local church. He was a wonderful speaker but knew that he lacked an essential skill. He'd hold a Bible in his hand for show, but he couldn't read. He could recite many of the verses he had learned as a child… but he lived in fear that he would be called upon to actually read from the page.

"The pastor keeps asking me to speak in church," he said to Mary.

"And you do a fine job of it," replied Mary.

"Well, I do the best I can," he said as he looked to the ground. "But," he added, searching for words. Mary looked at him in puzzlement. He again said, "but…"

Just then, Mary's mother came from around the corner of the room. "For goodness sake, just say it. Your stepfather is concerned because he can't read. And for a man who can ramble on for hours over a single line of **scripture**, I am amazed he can't just come out and ask you for help."

Mary jumped from her chair and hugged him. "Of course, I'll help you read. Anyone can do it, and someone as smart as you will have it down in no time." And Mary did just that, teaching him secretly in their home.

Mary was right about her stepfather; he was a smart man. Smart enough to learn anything he set his mind to and smart enough to let someone help him improve.

Soon, he wasn't just holding the Bible in his hand, he was reading it aloud. And people began to notice. Of course, they didn't have to ask how he gained his new-found skill. They knew the story of Mary's mother sending her off to Alexandria for an education.

Soon, others in the community were asking for Mary's help. And helping others was in Mary's very nature. She loved to share what she knew and wouldn't have dreamed of saying no.

Officially, Mary made her living by sewing for others. Unofficially, she was Hampton's finest reading teacher.

But how did she do it? After all, she could be imprisoned, fined, and even beaten if she were caught. It was all there in the laws of Virginia. And there were Vigilante Committees across the state making sure those laws were followed.

Maybe she was in her sewing room, with a dress on her lap. Another lady might come over with some sewing of her own to do. They are sitting in the room working. And all the while, Mary's "sampler" from school is hanging on the wall showing the entire alphabet.

"Do you see that apple, there on the wall? Now look right above it. Do you see that symbol? That's the letter 'A.' The word 'apple' begins with the letter 'A.'"

As her friend continues to sew, she says, "'A' is for apple."

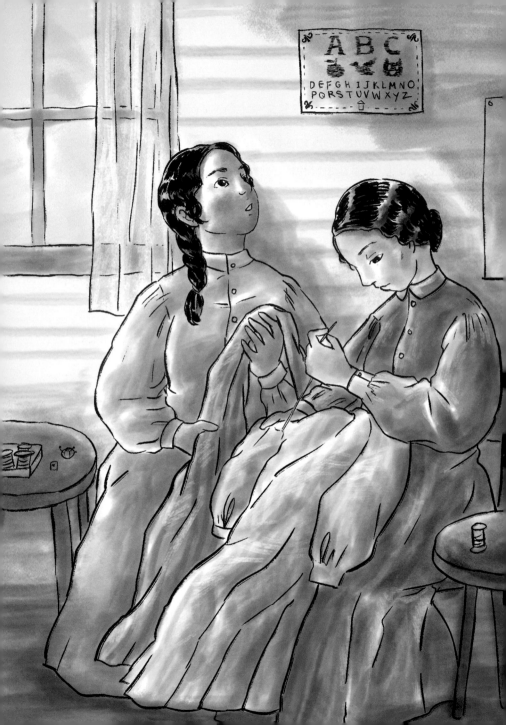

It may have started that way, but later they might have gotten a little braver and hidden a slate or writing tablet under their sewing. They could pull it out to write a word or to read a sentence Mary had written. They could easily hide it if someone else came by.

Word got around that Mary had great skills as a teacher, and many were happy for her work. Still, it was important to keep her teaching a secret.

Soon, the need expanded beyond a single student and the risk of being caught increased. That was a risk Mary was willing to take.

The Big Boat

Sam is holding Mary's Bible and is in the middle of reading a story. His little sister stares out the drawn curtains of the back door leading to the kitchen. She is making sure no one comes in unexpectedly.

Other children are sitting nearby, listening.

"So make yourself an **ark** *of* **cypress** *wood… The ark is to be three hundred cubits long, fifty cubits wide and thirty cubits high,"* read Sam.

"A cubit is about one and half feet long, so that's a really big boat!" said Mary.

"At least as big as a barn," said one of the children who marveled to hear the story.

"Keep reading, Sam," said Mary as she leaned over his shoulder. Sam was one of Mary's most skilled readers.

"You are to bring into the ark two of all living creatures, male and female, to keep them alive with you."

"Two of every animal, Miss Mary!"

"That's what it says," she replied. "What animals do you think were on that boat?"

"Ducks!" said one child. "Chickens!" said another. "Cats!" said another. "And cows and mules and horses and dogs!"

"I hope they're nice dogs," said one little girl.

"I'm sure they were nice dogs. Mr. Noah would insist on it," said Mary.

"You'd need a big room to hold all those animals."

"You'd need a big boat to hold all the food!" said another."

"Somebody's coming!" yelled the girl looking out of the window.

"Okay, you know what to do. And remember, if anyone asks any questions, I'll answer," said Mary.

Instantly, the group sprang into action. Mary grabbed her Bible. The children quickly erased their slate boards on which they had written letters. They placed the slates in a drawer.

There is a knock on the door and Mary goes to answer it. "It's Sarah. You're late young lady."

"I got here as soon as I could," she replied.

The group breathed a sigh of relief. But one of the boys frowned a bit. "Building a boat bigger than a barn to hold all those animals. Nobody could do that!"

"I'll bet Mr. Peake could," said the little girl.

"And just what do you know about Mr. Peake?" said Mary with a bit of a blush.

"Everybody knows Mr. Peake can build a boat, or sail off any where he wants to catch a haul of fish, or tie any kind of knot there is," said one of the boys.

"And he's always asking about you," said the little girl.

"Asking about me?" said Mary.

"Yes," said another girl. "He asks if you've been by to see us. What dress you were wearing. If you had on that perfume that makes you smell so pretty."

"Well, I don't think my perfume or my dress is any of Mr. Peake's business," said Mary, "and I certainly hope you tell him that if he ever comes around asking about me again. Now, we better run along before we all get into to trouble."

"Thank you, Miss Mary!" came one by one as they snuck out the back door of the house. But before she left, the little girl came back and whispered in Mary's ear.

"Shhh! I think Mr. Peake likes you," she said as she kissed Mary on the cheek.

"I think you're right," replied Mary as she gave out a smile.

Mary liked Mr. Peake as well. He had a winning smile that made him well liked by anyone who met him. Though he was born a slave, his hard work and clever ways helped him to receive his freedom.

That led to time as a merchant marine which led to a profitable career and eventually owning properties in Hampton.

Mary loved his strong arms and his rough hands that were weathered from working on the water. For his part, he loved the petite Mary. He admired her skills as a seamstress and thought her beautifully-created dresses made her look like a princess. Most of all, he admired her work as a teacher and was thrilled when she became his wife in 1851.

They were quite a couple and five years later, they were blessed with a daughter who they adored. They gave her the name Hattie but Mr. Peake always said, "She's as cute as a Daisy."

And soon, she was only known as Daisy.

Once Mary became a mother, she began to fully appreciate what her own mother had done for her. She realized that she had never loved anyone as much as her daughter and would do anything for her. She finally understood how hard it must have been to send Mary away for an education. Daisy could only

be taught in secret. And Mary could only dream of a day when her daughter could go to school out in the open.

Even more, America was changing quickly… and not for the good.

I'd Rather Be Dead!

By 1860, America was more divided than ever. **Abraham Lincoln** was elected President in November. He believed that the United States must remain united at any cost. There was more and more pressure between slaveholding states and free states and as more states joined the Union, there was pressure to keep those states free. This led to southern states deciding one by one to leave the United States of America and form their own country… the Confederate States of America. On May 23, 1862, Virginia **seceded** from the United States.

That same day, **Frank Baker, James Townsend, and Shepard Mallory** spent the day digging trenches and embankments in Norfolk in order to fight against Lincoln's Northern, Union soldiers. It was not by their choice that they put in this backbreaking work for the Southern, Confederate soldiers. They were enslaved men and had to do as they were ordered. But they also knew that their work would only hurt the very Northern soldiers who might be able to one day offer them freedom from the South. It was horrible enough to live every day as a slave, but to work tirelessly in the blazing sun against the only hope for freedom was too much.

They heard the soldiers talking. They knew that Virginia had declared itself separate from the United States earlier in the day.

"When all these trenches are done, I hear they're going to send us down to South Carolina or Georgia to dig more trenches," said Baker.

"And we'll never see our families again," said Townsend.

"We've got to get across the water to that fort, that's our only chance," said Mallory.

Hampton's Fort Monroe was a little piece of Northern territory in the midst of the South. Situated at the tip of the Chesapeake Bay it offered wide views of the bay. It

was a clear target for the Southern Confederates.

That night, the three brave men slipped past Southern soldiers guarding the camp. They had to be careful, if the dogs heard them and started barking, they'd be caught for sure.

They headed straight for the waters of Hampton Roads that separated Norfolk and Fort Monroe. The three looked at one another for a moment, nodded their heads and carefully lowered a small boat into the water.

Slowly, and as cautiously as they could, they dipped the paddles into the water and stroked closer and closer toward the fort. The only sound louder than the drops of water falling off of their paddles was the pounding of their hearts as they got closer and closer to shore. At any moment, their overseers might notice they had escaped and would be after them with guns. On the other side of the water, an anxious Northern soldier might mistake them for a Southern soldier and shoot.

Frank whispered to the others, "There it is… if we can make it to the fort, we'll be free."

"Until they send us back," said Mallory.

"I'd rather be dead than dig another trench," said Townsend.

"And I'd rather be dead than to live another day as a slave," followed Baker.

Somehow, after what seemed like hours, they had made it across the water. They slowly raised their arms high in the air and stopped moving as they saw two Union soldiers approaching quickly with their guns drawn.

"What do we do with 'em?" asked the first one breathlessly.

"I don't know. We'll wait and see what **Major General Butler** says."

General Butler Makes a Ruling

The next morning, Baker, Townsend, and Mallory plead their case before Major General Benjamin Butler. He immediately reviewed several books in his office and was well-prepared to speak with Confederate Major **John B. Cary** who appeared outside the fort that afternoon.

Cary, holding a white flag of **truce** said, "Benjamin Butler, give me back those slaves… you have no right to keep them."

"Not so fast, not so fast. Maybe I don't have to give them back," he said. "As I understand it, you claim Virginia is no longer a part of the United States of America."

"That may be true. Virginia is no longer part of the Union. But there's still the runaway slave act! It says you have to give me back those slaves."

"If you are claiming to no longer be part of the United States, how can you come here asking me to treat you like a United States citizen?" said Butler.

"There are rules, even in war. Even a second-rate political appointee should know that," replied Cary.

"It's true I may not be the greatest soldier in the Union army," smiled Butler. "But I'm a darn good lawyer. Now Mr. Cary, even though I may disagree with you, you consider these slaves property, right?"

"Of course, they belong to Colonel Charles K. Mallory."

"Hold on now. You could make these slaves do practically anything you tell them to, right?"

"Of course, I can," Cary said matter-of-factly. "They're slaves. They do what they're told."

"You could have them plant crops, tend to animals?"

"Matter of fact, they were digging trenches for my troops until they ran away," said Cary.

"Digging trenches to fight against me? Well, isn't

that interesting. Like you said, Mr. Cary, there ARE rules, even in war. And I've been reviewing those rules carefully. It seems I CAN take any of your property that you can use against me in the war."

"You can't do that," yelled Cary.

"I certainly can," replied Butler. "And let me be absolutely clear. If any slave makes it here to Fort Monroe, they will not be returned to the South."

"Benjamin Butler… You have not heard the last of me," Cary shouted as he stormed away.

Burn it to the Ground!

It was amazing how quickly the word spread. In Washington, D.C., Congress confirmed that Major General Butler could protect any enslaved people who fled to Fort Monroe. These people became known as **Contraband** Slaves. Contraband, or illegal, because they were being used to help fight against the United States.

Fort Monroe soon became known as "**Freedom's Fortress**" as enslaved people from across the South raced to the small fort. As the number of freed people increased, their numbers spilled into the surrounding community.

"Slaves are running up and down the streets. Next thing you know they'll be living in my home! Using my dishes!" cried one resident.

"Oh, that will never happen!" replied her friend.

"Never happen? Never happen! I've heard a rumor

that President Lincoln is going to turn the whole town over to the slaves!"

"Don't worry about that. My husband assures me that his troops will burn it to the ground first!"

And burn it to the ground they did. On August 7, 1861, 500 Confederate soldiers lit torches, and soon all of downtown Hampton was ablaze.

Despite the noise and chaos, Mary read to Daisy the story of brave Joshua in the Bible who was reminded time and again, "No matter what, remain courageous." And Daisy stayed strong. They remained strong when their home caught fire. Fortunately, they were able to make it safely to Mary's mother's home.

The next morning, Mary and Thomas walked through downtown Hampton to see the damage. Thomas and Mary had lost two properties and much furniture and many possessions in the fire… but they were safe.

They remained totally silent as they looked at the homes, schools, and shops… all reduced to black, soot-covered rubble.

They knew the war would be difficult, but could hardly imagine that people were so angry that they would burn down their own homes, their own livelihoods, the future success of their own children rather than consider change.

Even Mary, ever the optimist, had tears in her eyes as she viewed the destruction. She had told Daisy that they would be protected and all would be well. But now Mary wondered and worried. She worried until she turned the corner… beyond the toppled bricks and charred skeletal remains of buildings, one structure remained. St. John's Church was still standing. The peak of the building rose over the destroyed town and the sun sparkled brightly behind the pointed building top which still stood strong.

Then Mary remembered a verse she had memorized long ago… *"All things will work to the good of those who trust the Lord."*

Mary took the sunshine behind the top of the building as a sign that all would be well.

School is in Session

There was a sharp knock on the door. When Mary Peake's mother answered it there was a tall man, dressed all in black, standing on the porch. Her mother had never seen the man before.

"Good day. Are you Mrs. Peake?" said the man.

Her mother was cautious, especially since the burning of the town. Why would this white man be asking for her Mary?

"I'm looking for Mrs. Mary Peake, the teacher," he said, "They told me I could find her here."

Oh, no. Word of Mary's teaching had gotten out. Perhaps she'll be arrested. "I'm not Mary Peake and I don't know where she is."

Just then, Daisy came running out from the parlor. And before her grandmother could stop her, she blurted out, "That's my mother. She's in the side yard planting turnips. I'll show you."

Before Mary's mother could stop them, they were headed to the side yard.

"So, you are Mary Peake?" he said, "I've been searching everywhere for you."

Mary stood up from the garden. She had a small shovel in her hand and looked to her mother out of concern.

Sensing that they were both uncomfortable, he took off his hat, "Please forgive me. Where are my manners? I haven't introduced myself. I'm **Lewis Lockwood**. Reverend Lewis Lockwood. I forgot I wasn't wearing my preacher's collar."

"Reverend?" said Mary. "Oh, please come in."

Reverend Lockwood explained that he was with the American **Missionary** Association. Once General Butler had made his ruling and people started swarming to Fort Monroe, he came down to help in any way he could.

"General Butler said one of his top priorities is to start

teaching all of the children who are coming here how to read, so I started looking for a teacher. The moment I said the word 'teacher' to anyone around the fort they said, 'You need to see Mary Peake.'"

"See, everyone knows about you," her mother said.

"As more and more people are freed, it is important that they have the skills to survive. They have to get an education. They have to be able to read. Mary Peake, I need you to teach them."

Before Mary could say "yes" he added, "Of course, we'll provide the books and of course, it pays a little. I must admit the **stipend** isn't much."

"Real school books? I don't know what to say," Mary exclaimed.

"Say yes, mamma!" said Daisy.

"Of course. Yes! There's not much room here for students. I don't know that we could fit more than ten here in the parlor. And this isn't my house. I wouldn't want to endanger my family."

"You don't understand, Mrs. Peake. Because you are here by 'Freedom's Fortress' you could call this Union Territory. You can now teach out in the open."

"Out in the open?" she cried. "That's all my husband and I have been praying for… to teach Daisy and other children out in the open."

Little did Mary realize that when Reverend Lockhart said "out in the open," he literally meant "out in the open." While they were waiting to find a suitable space to teach, Mary was to start right away. Instead of a classroom, she was to teach under a giant oak tree near the water… right by the center of town. And this wasn't just any oak tree, it was a tree that took root in 1831, the same year Virginia had passed that law forbidding reading instruction to any black person in the state.

The first day of classes, Mary set up under that giant oak tree. An officer stood guard at a distance.

For the longest time, no one came. Perhaps they hadn't gotten the word. Or perhaps they were fearful

that it was all a trap to find and punish all who could read.

Finally, Thomas appeared with Daisy. He told her, "Hurry on now. What would it look like, you being late on the first day of school?" Daisy ran to her mother and they sat down to start their lessons. Then, from around the bushes and reeds, a little boy appeared. His clothes were threadbare. He looked, anxiously at first. Then his mother stepped forward and gave him a push. Mary's smile told him it was okay to come join them.

And soon there was another and another. Five in total that first day. Mary was not discouraged at all. "We're planting seeds," she told her daughter. "If just one person learns to read, they can teach another and another."

Five children turned to ten. Ten to twenty. And then there were fifty students.

"We are so lucky to be here," said Mary at the start of one lesson.

A little boy responded, "Lucky? Your house burnt to the ground. How is that lucky?"

"But I'm here with all of you. And each of you are learning to read. And when you can read, a whole world opens up. So read! Learn all you can. Learn new skills. Learn of your *ancestors*… Where they came from. How they lived. You have an opportunity that children across the country can't even dream of."

Mothers and fathers who wanted to help their children approached Mary. But how could they help if they couldn't read? Soon, Mary was teaching children in the morning and adults at night.

The Pageant

Reverend Lockwood was good on his word. He found a space near Mary's tree as it now was called. It was a two-story building where Mary could teach downstairs and she and her family could live upstairs.

Her students were doing so well at reading, learning, and memorizing that it was decided that a big celebration was in order. On December 25th they would have a Christmas Day party as a reward for what they had accomplished.

The event would end with a pageant of songs, readings, and **recitations**. When she wasn't teaching, Mary made costumes for the children. Daisy helped with the angel costume. She was starting to show some of her mother's gift with a sewing needle.

Finally, the big day arrived and the room was filled with happiness and warmth. It had been an amazing year filled with fear, disaster, tragedy, and then unexpected joy and opportunities. A year ago, this gathering would have been unthinkable. And yet, here they were. Reading, singing, sharing stories, and most of all, enjoying the company of one another.

The activity, hard work, and long hours finally caught up with Mary. As the children presented their pageant, she went to the back of the room and sat down. Thomas came and stood beside her.

Finally, it was Daisy's turn. She walked onto the makeshift stage, dressed in her angel costume. She had little wings attached in the back and a halo on her head. The room filled with wondrous silence as she appeared.

Then, she surprised her mother and the entire crowd as she sang every verse of "I Want to Be an Angel." Her sweet and beautiful voice was truly angelic as it projected through the room.

"I Want to Be an Angel
And with the Angels Stand
A Crown Upon My Forehead
A Harp Within My Hand
I Never Should Be Weary
Nor Ever Shed a Tear
Nor Ever know a Sorrow
Nor Ever Feel a Fear."

Mary looked up at Thomas and grabbed his hand. All the hard work was worth it. She smiled and he squeezed her hand. As tired as she was, Mary was so happy. This was, by far, the best Christmas ever.

Emancipation

It was an especially brisk day and there was excitement in the air. Anticipation of something long-hoped for.

"They've got it!" said one young man at the top of his lungs as he ran toward town. "Hurry up, they're gonna read it! They're gonna read it!"

As he turned the corner, he could see that the word had gotten out. It seemed like every member of the community was gathered around Mary's tree. Suddenly, one of Mary's adult students stepped forward and cleared his throat.

Abraham Lincoln, at great political cost, worked to push through an order, a **proclamation**. After so much sacrifice and so many dead, he was determined that there would be a positive outcome from the horrible war.

Under Mary's tree, many African Americans, some freed, some soon to be freed, heard these words, the Emancipation Proclamation, for the first time in the South:

"Now, therefore I, Abraham Lincoln, President of the United States, by virtue of the power in me vested as Commander-in-Chief... do order and declare that all persons held as slaves... are, and henceforward shall be free."

Around the tree, some raised their hands in praise. Some cried. A little way back, you can see Thomas and little Daisy. But you won't find Mary.

If you had asked Daisy where her mother was, she would tell you that her mother now has angel wings.

After the Christmas celebration, Mary had become quite ill. Before the war, she had contacted **tuberculosis**, a disease that made breathing difficult and drained her energy.

By January, she was so weak that she could only teach from her bed.

Mary's husband and mother begged her to stop teaching but to no effect. Mary insisted that as long as she had one breath left, she would keep teaching. She would keep planting seeds. And so, she kept going, until February 22, 1862, when she whispered goodbye to her family. She insisted that they would be together again one day and then she slipped away.

How she would have celebrated Lincoln's proclamation. How she would have been so proud that it was being read, in her community, to her neighbors, and by her students.

The Learning Tree Continues to Grow

The seeds that Mary planted didn't stop growing after Mary's death. In 1863, the Butler School was built beside Mary's Tree which was now better known as the Emancipation Oak.

The war ended in 1865. The next year, Brigadier General **Samuel Armstrong**, working with the American Missionary Association, built a larger school. Then, on April 1, 1868, he opened Hampton Normal and Agricultural Institute which has taught thousands of scholars including Booker T. Washington who went on to lead the Tuskegee Institute.

Under the leadership of Dr. William Harvey, the school has grown into Hampton University, graduating over 800 students a year. These students serve their communities as doctors, pharmacists, nurses,

engineers, and, of course, teachers.

Just two miles away, in 1961, the city of Hampton opened the Mary Peake School. Today, children of all races and economic backgrounds enter the school. It is the home of a dynamic and nurturing early childhood program that makes sure that every student has a solid background to begin their learning journey.

Mary would certainly be happy, and if she could speak to those children, she might say, "Read. Learn all you can. Make the most of today so that tomorrow you can make a difference in our world. Your community is counting on you and so am I."

Photos and More

A street named in Mary's honor in Hampton, Virginia.

Author photograph

This is the only known photo of Mary Peake.
The original is now in the archives of the
Hampton University Museum.

A "CONTRABAND" SCHOOL.

Dr. Lockwood wrote a small book about Mary after her death. Here are illustrations from that book.

Mary S. Peake

LITTLE DAISY.

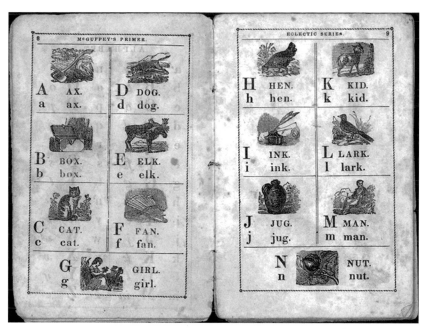

Library of Congress photo

The McGuffey Reader is an example of a text book (sometimes called a primer) that was used in Mary's time.

This is the song that Daisy sang at the Christmas Pageant in 1862. The unique version at the bottom is written in shape notes. The shapes indicate what tone to sing. This notation was used in some hymn books in the 1800's.

Top image "The Young Singer's Friend" from 1859. Bottom image is "The Christian Harp and Sabbath School Songster" 14th edition from 1875.

Photos courtesy of Hymnology.org

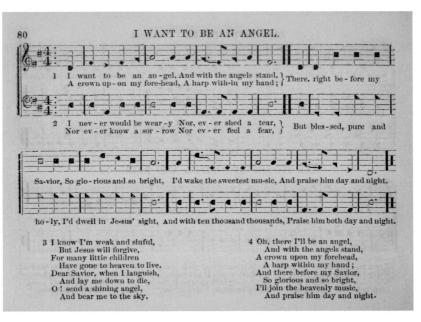

Here is a typical "sampler" from the 1800's. These were used to demonstrate a student's needlework.

And here's an example of dresses from the period. Notice all of the details.

Public domain image

Author photo, Hampton History Museum

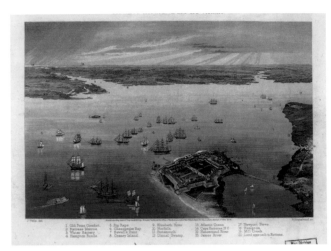

Here is a map of Fort Monroe from 1861.

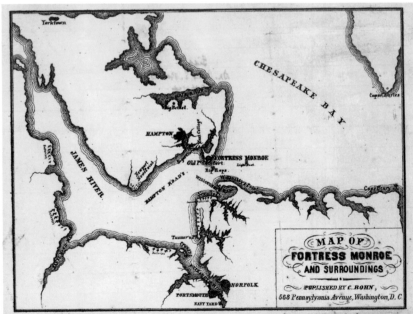

The burning of Hampton was news across the country.
St. John's is still standing in downtown Hampton,
with a new roof, of course.

ST. JOHN'S CHURCH
HAMPTON, VIRGINIA

THE OLDEST ANGLICAN PARISH IN
CONTINUOUS EXISTENCE IN AMERICA,
ESTABLISHED IN 1610. THIS IS THE FOURTH
CHURCH BUILT IN THE PARISH. IT WAS
ERECTED IN 1728 IN THE SHAPE
OF A LATIN CROSS. ITS WALLS ARE
TWO FEET THICK. THE BRICKS ARE
LAID IN FLEMISH BOND. ITS COMMUNION
SILVER BEARS THE HALLMARK 1618 AND
HAS BEEN TERMED "THE MOST PRECIOUS
RELIC IN THE ANGLICAN CHURCH IN
AMERICA". THESE VENERABLE WALLS HAVE
SUFFERED DURING THE REVOLUTIONARY WAR, THE
WAR OF 1812, AND THE WAR BETWEEN THE STATES.

You can visit Fort Monroe today.

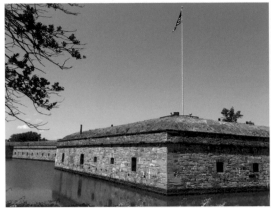

Author photos

President Barack Obama made Fort Monroe
a National Monument on November 1, 2011.

US Army photo   *Official White House Photo by Pete Souza*

Mary's tree, the Emancipation Oak, still stands at Hampton University.

Author photo, Hampton University

Jimmy Olivero photo.

Hampton University has grown into a huge campus.

Dr. William Harvey has led Hampton University since 1978. Under his leadership, the school has added Masters and Doctoral programs with a concentration on research, education, and medicine.

Judy Lowery photo

Author photos.

Mary fittingly rests beside
Thomas, under a beautiful tree in
Hampton. A historic marker at the
corner of Wine Street and Poplar
Avenue in Hampton notes her
accomplishments.

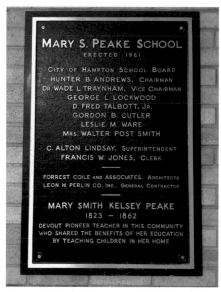

Mary Peake School was built in 1961 and now serves as the home of the Downtown Hampton Child Development Center.

Author photo.

Downtown Hampton Child Development Center photo

Rainbow Puppets' Mary Peake and Benjamin Butler were built by Pennsylvania puppet maker Jill Harrington. The costumes are by Iowa artist Regina Smith. The hand-crafted lace on the Mary Peake puppet is over 100 years old.

Judy Lowery photo

Compare the photo of Benjamin Butler with his puppet counterpart below.

Author and Public Domain photo

Abraham Lincoln was created by Hampton puppet maker Laura Huff and requires two puppeteers to operate.

Judy Lowery photo

Gerri Hollins, the founder of the Contraband Historical Society, provided the voice of Mary Peake for Rainbow Puppets. She is seen operating the Benjamin Butler puppet after the show's premiere and in the studio recording with her voice students.

City of Hampton photo

Our Mary Peake puppet being demonstrated on the "Round Robin" television program. The Rainbow Puppets have told the Mary Peake story to tens of thousands of children across Virginia, performing in schools, libraries, museums, and theaters.

Hampton Heroes

On January 21, 2019, the City of Hampton recognized several Hampton Heroes with a plaza at the Hampton Roads Convention Center. They include General Samuel C. Armstrong, Frank Baker, Maj. General Benjamin Butler, Gerri Hollins, Rev. Lewis Lockwood, Shepard Mallory, Mary S. Peake, and James Townsend.

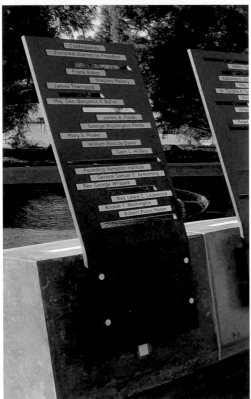

City of Hampton photos

Acknowledgements

I am especially grateful to the late Gerri Hollins, founder of the Contraband Historical Society. She shared much about both Mary Peake and her relatives who were contrabands. Gerri was a gifted teacher, composer, singer, and owner of a dog who could do math. (It's true! I saw him do adding and subtracting in a classroom at Francis Asbury School in Hampton.) Gerri later provided the voice of Mary Peake for our puppet productions.

Another member of the Contraband Historical Society is my former newspaper colleague, former Rainbow Puppeteer, and good friend Tony Gabriele. He generously reviewed this document before printing and offered significant insight.

Barbara Weaver's frank feedback and helpful criticism were proof that the Virginia Department of Education made the right choice when selecting her as History Teacher of the Year in the Gilder-Lehrman National Competition of 2004.

Dr. Jim Stensvaag, historian (retired) Casemate Museum of Ft. Monroe, editor of "From the Sea to the Stars" helped with the original stage production which formed the basis of this story.

The staff at the Hampton University Museum Archives were generous with their time and in allowing access to all material related to Mary Peake and the Emancipation Oak.

Chadra Pittman's discussion on the power of language at the Hampton History Museum was insightful and timely.

Thanks to Caitlin Flanagan, Olivia Hasan, Heather Livingston, Robin McCormick, Nancy Kent Swilley, Mayor Donnie Tuck, Marcy, and my parents for their generous assistance and support.

Bibliography

"Death of Mrs. Peak." American Missionary. April 1862

"A First Hampton Christmas." (adapted from "They Blazed the Trail") Hampton University Archives. December 1967.

Lockwood, Rev. Lewis C. Mary S. Peake: The Colored Teacher at Fortress Monroe. Boston, American Tract Society, 1862.

"Mrs. Mary Peake's School." Southern Workman. April 1884, 46.

Peake, Mary. "Letter from Mrs. Peake." American Missionary. December 1861, 288-289.

"Sabbath and Week-Day Schools." American Missionary. November 1861, 256.

Taylor, Kay Ann. "Mary S. Peake and Charlotte L. Forten: Black Teachers During the Civil War and Reconstruction." The Journal of Negro Education. 2005. Vol. 74. No. 2.

"Thomas D. Peake." Southern Workman. June 1897, 109.

While Mary Peake would have used the King James translation of the Bible, for ease of reading, quotes are from the New International Version.

"I Want to Be an Angel" written and composed by Sidney P. Gill. circa. 1854, Public Domain. (Courtesy of Hymnology.org)

Glossary

Abraham Lincoln – The 16th President of the United States. He signed the Emancipation Proclamation.

Alexandria – A portion of the District of Columbia which, during Mary's lifetime, was not considered part of Virginia as it is today.

Ancestors – Relatives who came before.

Ark – A very large boat, build by Noah and his sons in the Bible story.

Benjamin Butler – Union Major General who refused to return enslaved men to Virginia soldiers.

Contraband – Something prohibited by law.

Cypress – A dark green evergreen tree.

Frank Baker, James Townsend, and Shepard Mallory – Three enslaved men who fled Norfolk for Fort Monroe, becoming freed men.

"Freedom's Fortress" – The informal name given to Fort Monroe after enslaved people found freedom there.

Goliath – A giant warrior who was defeated by a much smaller, young boy named David in a Bible story.

Hampton, Virginia – Oldest continuously-occupied English settlement in the United States. The area includes Fort Monroe, the Emancipation Oak, and was Mary Peake's hometown.

Independent – Able to act or operate on its own.

John B. Cary – A Confederate Major who was using enslaved men to build trenches.

Lewis Lockwood – A missionary who came to help newly freed people at Fort Monroe.

Merchant – A seller of products.

Missionary – A person sent by a church to help or teach others.

Norfolk, Virginia – Mary's place of birth on the Chesapeake Bay, across the water from Hampton, Virginia.

Primer – A book to teach children to read.

Proclamation – An official announcement.

Recitations – Speaking from memory.

Samuel Armstrong — The Union Brigadier General who later formed Hampton Normal and Agricultural Institute, which became Hampton University.

Scripture – A passage from the Bible.

Seceded – To leave an alliance officially.

Separation – To take apart something that was once together.

Stipend – A payment for a service.

Truce – An agreement not to fight.

Tuberculosis – A disease that usually affects the lungs.

Vigilante – Someone taking the law into their own hands.

Virginia SOL Connections:

HIST 2.4; VUS 7 b,c,d; VUS 6 e; GOVT 3 a, b, e, f, GOVT 7 d; VS 7 a,b,c; VS 8 b

Mary was documented to have taught her stepfather how to read. We have found no records on how she taught before August of 1861 so we have fictionalized those accounts. Mary's assistance to the old man in Norfolk and receipt of his personal belongings at his death have been documented. Biographical information about him is fictionalized. Most records indicate that Mary's father was a white Englishman of means, though some records state that he was French.

The original stage productions which form the basis of this book were funded, in part, by grants from The York County Arts Commission, the City of Hampton, and Jamestown 400th Host Committee. Special thanks to the City of Williamsburg, James City County, and York County.

David Messick is the founder of Rainbow Puppet Productions. As a writer and composer, he has created dozens of original children's musicals including "Follow Me, a story of the Tuskegee Airmen" for the Smithsonian Institute National Air and Space Museum. He collaborated with the Tony Award winning director and designer of "The Wiz," Geoffrey Holder, to produce "Amazon Adventures." He's also worked on development projects for the Oprah Winfrey Show and the Disney Channel. He and his wife Marcy have been blessed with two amazing boys… Joshua and Luke.

www.davidmessick.com

Liu Light is an illustrator, writer, and art book maker based in New York City. A graduate of Virginia Commonwealth University, Light is involved with a number of community organizations for emerging marginalized artists. Notable collaborations include work with Shout Mouse Press and 3 Moons along with a number of east coast Art Book Fairs and Zinefests.

liulight.tumbler.com

Rainbow Puppeteers include James Cooper; Wesley Hutt; Alyssa Jones; David, Marcy, and Joshua Messick.

www.rainbowpuppets.com

Books from David Messick and Liu Light

"Creatures Great and Small"

"Mary Peake and the Mighty Acorn"

"Open a Book"

"The Tall, the Tough, and the Tiny"

Audio Programs by David Messick and the Rainbow Puppets

"The Amazing Adventures of Chessie the Manatee"

"From the Sea to the Sky"

"Jonah"

"The Mother Goose Traveling Rock and Roll Show"

"A Pirate Party"

"The Really Big Dinosaur Show"

"Toyland!"

"The Wetland Revue"

"The Wright Brothers – See Us Fly!"

Available at Amazon.com, iTunes,
RainbowPuppets.com,
DavidMessick.com